Meet the Saints From A-Z
A Child's Introduction to the Saints

Amy Schisler and
Judy MacWilliams

Bozman, MD 2022

$\mathcal{D}$ear Readers,

Do you ever wonder about the saints and who they were? Some of them were children like you, and others were teenagers or adults who lived their lives for God.

Have you heard some of the heroic stories about the saints and asked yourself, how is that possible?

St. Luke tells us "All things are possible with God." There are some remarkable stories of saints who were once children, just like you. These stories might help you see the saints more clearly in your mind and inspire you to try to be like them.

Note to Parents: Included on each page is a discussion question for you and your children to help them better understand how they can be like the saints. We encourage you to talk to your children about living like the saints and following their actions and examples. To help you with your conversations, a glossary has been added to the back of the book.

What is a saint?

A saint is someone who has died and gone to Heaven. Some people think that a person who goes to Heaven becomes an angel, but this is not correct. Angels are not people, but since they are in Heaven, we can say that they are saints, like St. Michael or St. Gabriel.

So, what is the difference between someone you know who has gone to Heaven and someone like St. Patrick or St. Luke or St. Teresa of Calcutta?

Well, for the past 2000 years, the Catholic Church has announced that people are known to be in Heaven because they died for their faith or because they performed miracles. This makes them Canonized Saints. There are four steps the Church takes before a person is called a Canonized Saint.

After a person dies, a request is made to the Vatican asking that the person be a saint, explaining how the person lived a very holy life. Once approved, the *Congregation for the Causes of the Saints* at the Vatican investigates the person's life. If the person was very holy, he or she may be declared *"venerable."*

Next, a person is named *"blessed."* If a person gave his or her life for Christ and died for Him, he or she is called a martyr and may be *"beatified"* and named *"blessed"* without any further investigation. If he or she was not martyred, people may pray to the person asking for a miracle to occur. If miracles are proven, the person may be *"canonized"* and declared a saint.

After all these things happen, the Pope announces that the person is holy and is in Heaven, watching over and guiding us. People may pray to that saint for help. Churches, schools, and other places or organizations may be named after the saint.

The Church does not create saints. It announces that God has made the person a saint by granting them entrance into Heaven. Many saints are patrons, meaning they, with the permission of God, can assist certain people or places with their needs.

Saints help people through something called *intercession*. An intercession is prayer that we send through someone else for help. It's like asking a friend to mail a letter for you since they are already going to the post office. Saints are already in Heaven with God and are close to Him. They can talk to Him and ask Him to help us. It's like asking your mom to help you convince your dad to give you something you want. You can ask your dad, and you should, but your mom can help him make his decision. Everything we ask, if we are praying to saints, should be asked in the name of Jesus.

We could pray to St. Isadore, the patron saint of farmers, "St. Isadore, please ask God to send us rain for our crops. We ask this in Jesus's name. Amen." We could pray to St. Richard Pampuri, the patron saint of doctors, "St. Richard, please help my friend's doctor make him well. I ask this in the name of Jesus."

Saints are always there for us, ready to take our prayers to Jesus just like we are always there for our friends and family to help them with their needs. When you pray for someone on earth, you are being just like the saints in Heaven.

Meet the Saints From A-Z

St. Agnes (291-304)

Patron Saint of the Girl Scouts

Agnes was a strong voice in the rights of young girls who were sometimes taken from their parents to live and work outside their family. When Agnes was a little girl, some men tried to take her.

Agnes fought her captors while praying for help. As one man tried to attack her, the Lord struck him blind. Later, Agnes prayed for him, and his sight was restored.

Can you pray for someone who has hurt you?

Dear St. Agnes,
Give us the strength to be a person of
courage, confidence, and character.
Amen.

St. Benedict (480-547) and St. Scholastica (480-543)

Patron Saints of brothers and sisters

Benedict and Scholastica were twins in Rome who dedicated their lives to God. Benedict left the city and moved to the country where he founded the Benedictine Order of Monks.

Scholastica became a nun and lived a simple life of holiness. They were able to see each other one time each year. Sick and dying, Scholastica prayed to God to keep her brother with her a little longer. A sudden storm prevented him from leaving.

How can you be a better brother, sister, or friend?

Dear Saints Benedict and Scholastica, Help me to love my sisters and brothers as you both did. Amen.

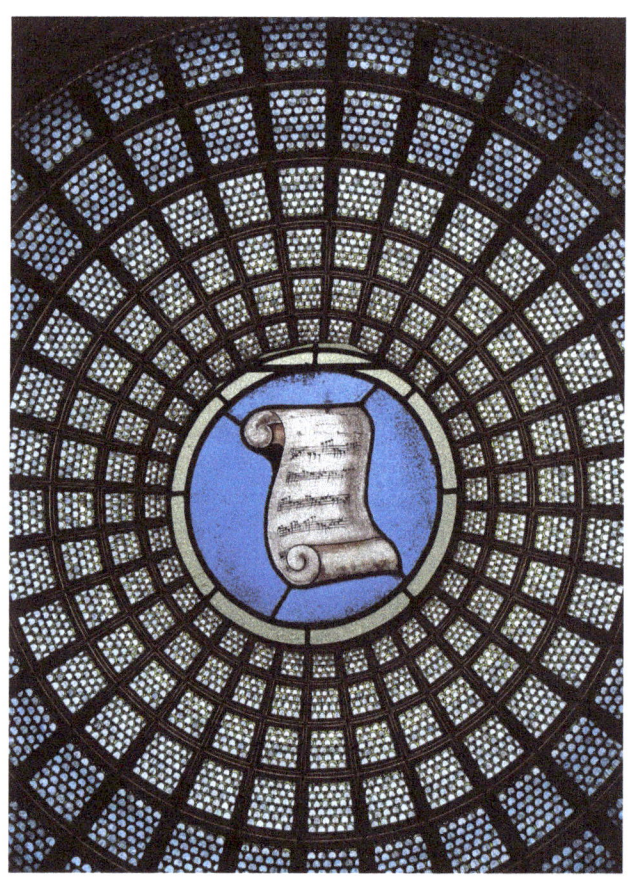

St. Cecelia (200-245)

Patron Saint of musicians

Cecelia used her beautiful voice to give praise to God. She sang to God on her wedding day and convinced her husband to be baptized. Her example and kindness helped convert many people in her homeland of Italy. She was martyred for refusing to turn away from her faith.

It was said that Cecelia could hear the heavenly music of angels in her heart.

What are the talents God has given you? Can you sing, dance, write, or play a sport really well?

Dear St. Cecilia,
Help me to use my talents for the glory of God and to lead others to you. Amen.

St. David (500-589)

Patron Saint of vegetarians and poets

Perhaps ahead of his time, David of Wales was a vegetarian who grew his own food and became a monk. He was a great preacher and writer who took good care of the environment.

David is often pictured with a dove on his shoulder. A legend tells us that a dove lifted David above the ground so he could be heard by the people.

"Do the little things in life," are his words to live by.

What can you do to take good care of the world around you?

Dear St. David,
Help me follow your words of
wisdom by doing small things to help
others. Amen.

St. Elizabeth Ann Seton (1774-1821)

Patron Saint of widows, orphans, and Catholic Schools

Elizabeth and her husband left England for America. They lived in New York and had five children before her husband died. Elizabeth moved her family to Maryland where she founded two schools for girls and began the Catholic School system in the United States.

Elizabeth founded the first convent in the United States and dedicated it to serving the children of the poor. She started the Sisters of Charity, one of the largest religious orders today.

How can you serve the poor around you?

Dear St. Elizabeth,
Help me to be a good student and to serve those in need. Amen.

St. Francis of Assisi (1181-1226)

Patron Saint of ecologists and animals

Francis was a very popular young man, always happy and charming. He was a born leader who often got into trouble. One night, he had a dream that God wanted him to be good, stay out of trouble, and pray more.

He preached to animals and once asked a wolf to stop hunting people. The wolf was instantly tamed and became the town pet. Francis helped bring many people to the Church, including several who became saints.

What can you do to help animals and people in need?

Dear St. Francis,
Help me to be good and to listen for your voice. Help me to be kind to people and animals. Amen.

St. George (201?-300)

Patron Saint of archers, soldiers, Boy Scouts, farmers, horseback riders, and plagues

George was born in Turkey and died in the Holy Land. He was a very brave soldier in the Roman Army, and legend says that George slayed a dragon to save a princess.

George's heroism made him popular with royalty. He is revered by kings in England, Greece, and many other countries.

Am I brave when I need to be, especially when God needs me to fight for Him?

Dear St. George,
Please help me to slay the things in my life that scare me, hurt me, or make me sick. Amen.

St. Helen of the Cross
(248-330)

Patron Saint of new discoveries

Helen, also known as Helena, wanted to find missing holy things. She spent years looking for the cross of Christ. She traveled to the Holy Land and began searching, with a team of excavators, the hill of Calvary where she found Jesus's cross. A Church was built on this site and is visited by millions of people every year.

Helen also helped the poor by giving them her money and her time.

What are some things that are so important to you that you would work really hard to find if they were lost?

Dear St. Helen,
Help me to help those who have lost their way. Amen.

THEOLOGIA

St. Isadore of Seville
(1070-1130)

Patron Saint of farmers and the Internet

When Isadore was a little boy in Spain, he had a hard time in school. Upset that he was not as smart as his brothers, he ran away from home. In the woods, he saw a rock with water dripping on it. He noticed the water was very slowly wearing away the rock. He understood that it sometimes takes a long time and a lot of work to achieve success. He went home and studied hard and was known as the smartest man of his time. He became a writer and teacher.

Do you take your time and work carefully on your schoolwork?

Dear St. Isadore,
Help me to remember that hard work always pays off. Remind me never to give up trying. Amen.

St. José Gabriel: The Cowboy Priest (1840-1914)

Patron Saint of priests and Córdoba, Argentina

José entered the seminary to become a priest at the age of 16. He was a parish priest in the Great Highlands of Argentina, an area that was so large, José had to ride a horse long distances to care for the people of his church. He dressed like a real cowboy in his hat, boots, and riding clothes.

José built post offices, telegraph offices, schools, and roads so his parish could communicate with the world. He died at an old age.

How far do you think you could go to spread the Word of God?

Dear St. José,
Help me to always find a way to get to those in need. Amen.

St. Kateri (1656-1680)

Patron saint of the environment

Kateri was a native Algonquin-Mohawk Indian born in New York state. At the age of 19, she caught a disease called smallpox that left her beautiful face scarred. Her tribe shunned her, and she left for Canada.

While in Canada she converted to Catholicism. She lived a pious and holy life and created a small chapel in the woods where she prayed. On her deathbed, at the age of 24, her face was restored to its beauty. She is known as the "Lily of the Mohawks."

Have people ever made fun of your looks or been mean to you? How did you respond to them?

Dear St. Kateri,
Help me to respect our land and its
resources, to use them wisely, and leave
a legacy of holiness. Amen.

*B*l. Lucia (1907-2005)

Lúcia of Fátima was born in 1907 in Portugal. When she was ten, she and her cousins, Jacinta and Francisco Marto, were visited by the Blessed Mother once a month for six months. At the time, they did not know the woman was Mary, but they listened to her and prayed the Rosary every day as she asked.

Following Mary's instructions, Lúcia learned to read and write so that she could write down everything about the visits. Lúcia became a nun and lived until she was 98 years old. She awaits canonization to become a saint.

Do you know how to pray the Rosary?

Dear Blessed Lúcia,
Help me to do as I'm told and to tell
people about Jesus and His Mother.
Amen.

St. Margaret of Scotland
(1045-1093)

Patron Saint of large families and Scotland

When Margaret was 18, her family was on the way to England when they were shipwrecked off the coast of Scotland. They were rescued and became friends with the king.

King Malcolm and Margaret fell in love and got married. They had 8 children. They prayed together, gave money and food to the poor, and built many churches. Margaret was loved by her people.

What can you do to show your family how much you love them?

Dear St. Margaret,
Help me to love my family and take care of them and the poor of the world. Amen.

St. Nicholas (270-343)

Nicholas is the patron saint of children, altar servers, sailors, and merchants

There are many stories and legends about St. Nicholas. It is believed he came from Greece and traveled the world. On one of his travels to the Holy Land, a fierce storm came over the ship. Nicholas prayed for the waves to calm, and they did.

Nicholas secretly gave money and gifts to people in need, often dropping apples and coins down chimneys. He was a kind man who loved to give gifts to those in need.

How can you be like St. Nicholas?

Dear St. Nicholas,
Help me to do good deeds and ease the worry of others as they face storms and rough seas in their lives. Amen.

St. Olga of Kiev (890-969)

Patron Saint of Kiev

Olga was the princess of Kiev when the Ukraine region was part of Russia. She became the ruler of Kiev after her husband died. After a trip to Constantinople, she returned to Kiev as a baptized Christian.

Olga was the first member of royalty in Russia to become a Christian. She brought the Orthodox Catholic faith to the region, and it is still the main religion of Ukraine today.

Have you ever asked your parents about the day you were baptized?

Dear St. Olga,
Help us to spread the word of
God's love to others. Amen.

St. Philomena (291-304)

Patron Saint of infants and children

Philomena was a young princess who dedicated her life to God by healing sick children. When she was 13, she was to be forced into marriage with an older emperor, but she refused. The emperor was angry and tried to harm her.

He ordered his archers to aim their arrows at Philomena, and she prayed to God for help. The arrows turned around and hit the archers instead. Some say the archers then became Christians.

When have you been afraid? Did you pray for God to help you?

Dear St. Philomena,
When we fear the worst, let us trust in God that he will turn things around for us. Amen.

*B*l. Signor (1890-1959) and Signora Quattrochhi (1894-1965)

Luigi and Maria Quattrochhi were the first modern couple to be beatified together. They lived in Rome where Luigi was a lawyer. Maria was a professor and writer before becoming a nurse to care for soldiers in World War II. They had four children.

Luigi and Maria started many Catholic organizations for men and women and led Scout troops for poor children. They are awaiting canonization to be saints.

What are some ways you might be able to work for God and His Church when you're older?

Dear Blessed Luigi and Maria,
Help me to lead a holy life, always
serving God by helping others. Amen.

*S*t. Richard Pampuri (1897-1930)

Patron Saint of doctors and surgeons

Richard became a doctor and served in World War I. After the war, he went home to Italy. He gave free health care to those in need, especially dental care.

He is credited with several miracles, including the restoration of sight to a young boy, Manuel. Richard suffered from poor health and was unable to become a priest, so he joined another religious group and spent his life working with the less fortunate.

Has there ever been something you wanted to do but couldn't? What did you do about it?

Dear St. Richard Pampuri,
Help me to find ways to help others even if it is not my top wish. Amen.

St. Sebastian (200-288)

Patron Saint of archers, athletes, and sufferers from plagues and pandemics

Sebastian was a soldier in the Roman Army. As a captain in the Army, he secretly converted many other soldiers to Christianity. He was sentenced to death, shot with dozens of arrows, and left for dead. A Christian woman nursed him back to health. He was later beaten and died.

In 680, the plague arrived in Rome. The citizens prayed to Sebastian, and they did not get sick. He is now known as The Protector Against Plagues.

Are you an athlete? Do you pray for safety before your games or matches?

Dear St. Sebastian,
Protect me from harm when I play sports or run around with my friends. Amen.

MUSICA

Sister Thea (1937-1990)

Thea was born in Mississippi, the granddaughter of slaves. She is the first Black woman to join the Secular Franciscans. She used her gift of singing and storytelling to teach about her faith. She recorded songs, published hymnals, and promoted Black music in the church. She helped found the National Black Sisters Conference.

Thea has been endorsed for sainthood by the U.S. Catholic Bishops. She said this daily prayer, "to live until I die, to live fully." She continued her work until she died in 1990.

What do you think it means to "live until I die"?

Dear Sister Thea,
Teach us how to pray and serve others, to live until we die, and to live fully. Amen.

*S*t. Ursula of Ledóchowska (1865-1939)

Patron Saint of girls, orphans, and educators

Sister Ursula, whose birth name was Julia, was born in Austria, the fifth of ten children, to a Polish Count and Countess. Her parents both died when she was young. When Julia was 21, she took her vows and became Sister Maria Ursula but was known as Sister Ursula.

In 1907, she opened the first college dormitory for girls. Later, she founded schools and orphanages for girls. When she was 55, Sr. Ursula founded the Ursuline Order of Nuns. She died at 74 with her Rosary in her hand.

Do you say your prayers every night?

Dear St. Ursula,
Help me to open my heart and my door to those needing a home. Amen.

*B*l. Victoria Rasoamanarivo
(1848-1894)

Victoria was born in Madagascar, the granddaughter of the Ruler. At the age of 15, she was baptized and married at the age of 17. There was tremendous pressure by the rulers to convert to another faith, but Victoria refused.

Since Victoria was considered a member of the royal family, she had more freedom than other Catholics. She used her freedom to keep open the Catholic schools and churches and was able to stop the forced conversions and murders of over 21,000 Catholics throughout the capital city and surrounding countryside. She was beatified by Pope John Paul II.

Has anyone been mean to you because of your religion?

Dear Blessed Victoria,
Help me to help others and to stay
faithful even if someone tries to stop me.
Amen.

St. Wenceslas (907-929)

Patron Saint of the Czech Republic, Poland, and justice for all

You may have heard the Christmas carol about Good King Wenceslas and wondered if he was a real person. The Good King was actually Duke of Bohemia, a region of the Czech Republic where dukes, not kings were in charge.

Wenceslas was a baptized Christian who became the Duke when he was just a little boy, so his mother ruled until he was 18. He was a kind leader who helped the poor, but some people were unhappy that Wenceslas was a Christian, and they killed him so that a new ruler could be chosen.

What can you do to spread kindness?

Dear St. Wenceslaus,
Help me to be a good leader who is kind to others. Amen.

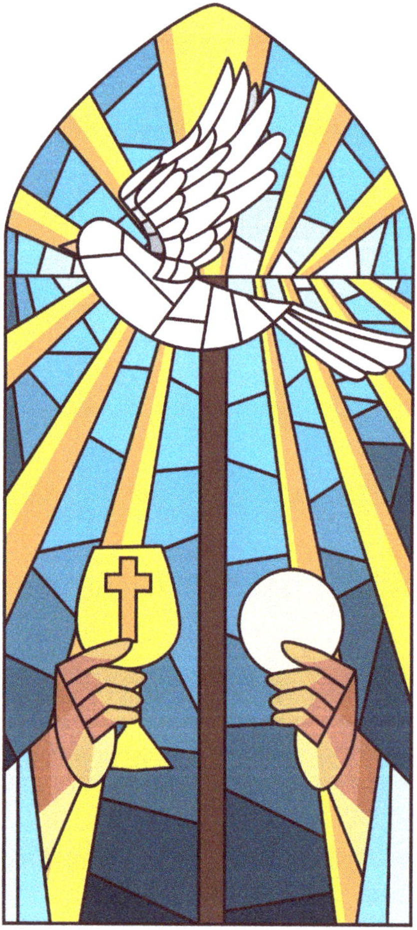

St. Francis Xavier (1506-1552)

Patron Saint of missions

Francis Xavier was born in Spain and did his religious studies in Paris where he became a priest and co-founded the Society of Jesus.

His mission was to travel to far-away Asia, Japan, and India. While in India he was credited with baptizing 20,000 people, going from village to village. He believed in evangelizing natives to continue spreading the Gospel. Francis hoped to reach China but died on his way there.

Do you tell other people about the Gospels?

Dear St. Francis Xavier,
Help guide us to travel our own paths in order to lead others to Jesus. Amen.

St. Yves (1253-1303)

Patron Saint of lawyers

Yves was a student of the law and graduated from the University of Paris. He practiced law, but he also studied the scriptures and became a monk with the Franciscans.

He continued his legal work by defending the poor and opposing the unjust taxes on citizens. His work for fair justice led him to be appointed a judge.

What is justice? How can you work for justice?

Dear St. Yves,
Show me how to fight for justice for all people. Help me to stand up and be counted. Amen.

St. Zygmunt Gorazdowski
(1845-1920)

Patron Saint of The Sisters of St. Joseph

Zygmunt was born in Ukraine in 1845 to a very religious family. As a child, he was often sick with a lung ailment, possibly asthma. He went to law school but felt called to the priesthood. He had lung problems his entire life.

As a priest, Zygmunt wrote books to help people understand God. He spent much of his time caring for the sick, poor, and homeless. He founded the Sisters of St. Joseph, women who work as nurses and teachers around the world.

Have you thought about being a nurse or teacher or someone else who helps others?

Dear St. Zygmunt,
Help me to take care of the poor and sick even when I am suffering myself. Amen.

Glossary

Baptism - The first sacrament that a Christian receives. It is the beginning of a life with Christ. Baptism happens when water is poured upon the head and the priest says, "I baptize you In the Name of the Father, Son, and Holy Spirit. Amen"

Beatified – The term used for a person who has been announced **"blessed"** and might someday be declared a saint.

Calvary - The place where Jesus died on the cross. Calvary is located in Jerusalem in the Holy Land.

Canonized – The term used for a person who has been declared a saint by the Catholic Church.

Conversion - When a person decides that he or she wants to become a Christian or when a Christian in another faith becomes a Catholic Christian.

Evangelizing - Spreading the Gospel to others, either by becoming a priest, monk, or nun, or when any person shares God's Word with others to help them become a Christian.

Holy Land - The areas in the country of Israel where Jesus lived and preached. He was born in Bethlehem, grew up in Nazareth, and traveled through Jerusalem, Cana, Samaria, and other towns, preaching love and forgiveness.

Holy Orders - One of the Seven Sacraments in which someone decides to become a priest, nun, or monk and turn his or her life over to God and receives "orders" to spread the Gospel to others.

Hymnals - The books that contain religious songs or hymns. Hymnals are used during the Mass or on other special occasions to praise God through music.

Martyr - A person who is killed for his or her belief in God. Most of Christ's Twelve Apostles and many of the early Christians died as martyrs. Martyrs automatically become saints.

Monk - A religious man who often spends his life in a place called a monastery. In the monastery, monks live a quiet life, praying, doing good deeds, writing, teaching, or even tending farms or caring for others. Some monks give up talking and remain in the same place their whole lives. They are recognized by their long, brown robes.

Orthodox – Catholic Churches in many parts of Eastern Europe. Some of these Churches believe the Pope is the Leader of the Church, but most believe the Eastern Orthodox Bishops are the Leaders. The Roman and Orthodox Churches share many saints.

Plague, The - A severe illness that spread throughout the world in the 1300s. Many people became sick and died.

Religious Orders – Groups of priests, nuns, or monks who dress alike and follow certain rules. Examples are the Benedictines, Franciscans, Sisters of Charity, Sisters of St. Joseph, The Society of Jesus, and the Ursulines. **Secular organizations** are groups that people can join to bring them closer to God without becoming priests, monks, or nuns. An example is the Secular Franciscans.

Rosary – A set of prayers given to St. Dominic by a vision of Mary in the 13th Century. A string of beads is used to say The Our Father, Hail Mary, and the Glory Be, plus the Apostles Creed and the Hail Holy Queen. When Mary appeared to the children in Fatima, she asked them to tell everyone to pray the Rosary every day.

Sacrament – A religious rite created by Jesus that helps us to be better people and go to Heaven. The Catholic Church celebrates seven sacraments over the course of a person's life—Baptism, Reconciliation, First Communion, Confirmation, Holy Orders or Marriage, and The Anointing of the Sick.

Seminary - A seminary is a school where men and women go to learn about God and study religious history and the sacraments. It's where men train to become priests.

Vatican, The – A small country, known as Vatican City State, contained in the city of Rome, Italy. It is where the Pope, the head of the Roman Catholic Church, lives and guides the church. Fewer than 2000 people live there, and most work for the Catholic Church

Venerable – A person who has met the first step to becoming a saint. They are people who have lived very holy lives.

About the Authors

Amy Schisler is a novelist, children's book author, spiritual writer, and blogger. Amy's novels have won numerous literary awards. She lives on the Eastern Shore of Maryland with her husband, daughters, and two dogs. When she's not writing, Amy can usually be found on a boat in the Chesapeake Bay or hiking in the Rocky Mountains, most often with a good book in her hand.

Judy MacWilliams grew up near St. Clement's Island where her ancestors arrived in 1634. Most of her relatives were watermen and farmers. Married to Richard for 59 years, they have three children, Amy, Scott, and Mike. Judy worked for the government and in education and wrote articles for several newspapers, including the Catholic Standard. Judy loves reading, gardening, and staying involved with her growing family that now includes seven grandchildren!

For more about the authors:
http://amyschislerauthor.com

http://facebook.com/amyschislerauthor
https://twitter.com/AmySchislerAuth
http://instagram.com/AmySchislerAuthor
https://www.goodreads.com/amyschisler

*B*y Amy Schisler:

Novels
A Place to Call Home
Picture Me
Whispering Vines
Summer's Squall
The Devil's Fortune
The Good Wine

Chincoteague Island Trilogy
Island of Miracles
Island of Promise
Island of Hope

Chincoteague Sunsets Trilogy
Seeking Tranquility

Buffalo Springs Series
Desert Fire, Mountain Rain

Under the Summer Moon

Children's Books
Crabbing With Granddad
The Greatest Gift

Spiritual Writing
The Devotional Alphabet
Stations of the Cross Meditations for Moms (with Anne Kennedy, Susan Anthony, Chandi Owen, and Wendy Clark)

www.ingramcontent.com/pod-product-compliance
Lightning Source LLC
Chambersburg PA
CBHW051553120626
46551CB00013B/1492